I0480410

The role of imagination in compulsive and impulsive purchasing behavior

Understanding Marketing through Philosophy

By Balbacha El Mehdi

Table of Contents

Abstract

Since 1950s, the humankind developed technologies that facilitated the production of goods and the freight traffic. Having occupied the role of privileged means of communication since their appearance during the late 20th century, social networks have been transformed into consumer incentive hub. With a perfect knowledge of each of its users, social medias are the perfect location for marketing experts to promote their product.

The expression "consumer society" was first employed by the American economist John Kenneth Galbraith. He identified the cause of this phenomenon as the "dependence effect", defining it as "a process by which wants are increasingly created by the process by which they are satisfied" (*The Affluent Society*, 1958). Goods are designed to have a short lifespan through both planned obsolescence and "innovation", so as to regularly renew consumption and therefore production, while services are limited in the time frame.

In a consumer society, individuals are pushed to purchasing and consuming as much goods / services as possible. Europe is the perfect example, based on the most representative factor of this phenomenon: consumer credit. A study lead by Crédit Agricole Consumer Finance (CACF) has published significant figures for three consecutive years of the current decade. Consumer credit has been growing from 2014 to 2016: +0,7% in 2014; +3% in 2015 and +4.4% in 2016.

The Cambridge Dictionary defines "consumerism" as "the state of an advanced industrial society in which a lot of goods are bought and sold". This behavior can result in deep dark feelings in which the consumer is trapped and from which he / she cannot flee. Finding the meaning of their existence in consumption, humans adopt automated behavior which consists in the excessive purchase of products, certainly useless sometimes.

Two types of buying behaviors are mainly considered by marketing experts when promoting their products: the compulsive and impulsive buying behaviors.

The former was proven to be caused by the obsessive-compulsive disorder (OCD), which was considered in religious texts in the earliest records before being observed as a part of the psychological field by the Freudian schools during the late 1800s. Obsessions are thoughts, images or ideas that a person isn't able to stop thinking about, causing him / her to feel anxious, whereas compulsions are the behaviors that the latter engages as to control those obsessive thoughts. As a result, that person ends up purchasing some goods / services that aren't necessary for the simple aim of controlling those thoughts.

On the other hand, impulsive buying behavior, that can be shortly referred to as "unplanned purchases", represents the second type of consuming behavior. In this case, the consumer is triggered by emotions and feelings, rather than by his / her thoughts. It is the case of 6% of the US population, with females being more affected than males. (Lejoyeux M, Richoux-benhaim C, Betizeau A, Lequen V, Lohnhardt H. *Money Attitude, Self-esteem, and Compulsive Buying in a Population of Medical Students.*).

Despite the fact that humans are endowed with a sharp rationality, a large part of them spends money in an exaggerated way, sometimes even against their own interests at the risk of being faced with a financial disaster. They are obedient to some marginal rules, and are enclosed in a dark envelope which is often called "Marketing".

How can this be explained? My tool to explain both consuming behaviors is philosophy. We'll talk about the role of imagination in the mutation of human consuming behavior over time, among others by mentioning the strong relationship between the notion of "money", "marketing" and "imagination". Two main authors will support my thesis, namely Aristotle and Immanuel Kant.

Both of them provide with statements that help us in understanding the role of imagination in both impulsive and compulsive buying.

Aristotle, in "*De Anima, book 3, Part3*", defines imagination as a faculty that relies within our power and that allows us recall an image. As for Kant, he believes that imagination is a faculty of <u>representation</u>: "imagination is a faculty for representing an object, even without its presence in intuition" (*Kant's Theory of the Imagination*).

Aside, we will base our study on another philosopher's statements (David Hume), as well as philosophical movements. Stoicism was founded in the early 3rd century BC by Zeno of Citium. It is famous for its claims according to which human happiness can be found in the acceptance of the present moment as it is, and not basing it on the desire of pleasure, or the fear of pain. Their philosophy is summarized as "the virtue is the only good". This implies that external things (money, health or pleasure as a general concept) are "materials for virtue to act upon", teaching us self-control as well as the overcoming of destructive emotions. This will be of great importance in understanding compulsive and impulsive shopping.

In the following paragraphs, you will see how central the role of imagination is in today's society's consuming behavior, based on philosophical writings.

Compulsive purchasing behavior

Senses in imagination

Senses play a primary role causing compulsive purchases. At the beginning of the third book of his writing *"On the Soul"* (350, B.C.E), the Greek philosopher Aristotle lists the five human senses: sight, hearing, smell, taste and touch. In the same book, also named *"De Anima"*, he states that imagination plays the pivot role in the thought process, which is stimulated by our senses. To sum, the Greek philosopher believes that all knowledge stems from our senses, which allow us to think thanks to *phantasia*.

Furthermore, it means that "thinking" and "imagination" are interdependent. These are two important aspects of the humankind on which we will base our study, and that is taken in consideration by companies during their marketing campaigns.

Indeed, we previously mentioned that OCD is the main cause of compulsive purchases because it triggers thoughts. For instance, a company that advertises its relaxing services (massage) will use a very quiet music (sense: hearing), to which it will add clean and soft white beds (sense: sight) if it's displayed on the TV. It would avoid promoting their services showing a dirty massage parlor with very shrill music as a background sound. Marketing experts are aware of the importance of senses when persuading a prospect to purchasing their goods / services.

As for Kant, he believes that imagination is a faculty of representation: "imagination is a faculty for representing an object, even without its presence in intuition" (*Kant's Theory of the Imagination*). Following this statement, the humankind can imagine whatever it wants, even things it has never seen, or used. To image this statement, Fabian Dorsch, in "*Routledge Handbook of Philosophy of Imagination*", mentions the hypothesis that anyone can imagine the backyard of a house without ever entering it.

Marketers will use customers' senses to persuade them, through the process of thought, that they actually need a certain amount of a specific item. This is how they become compulsive shoppers. The prospects (us) may either perceive the advertised product as being useful, or as a mean to satisfy their ego.

Following Aristotle's theory, senses would stimulate our imagination, which in turn will allow our thinking faculty to be engaged. This is how compulsive purchases are generated.

E-commerce and compulsive purchasing behavior

The attention of internet users has decreased over time due to the sudden increase of the amount of data shared online, including advertisings, since the beginning of the second millennial. Indeed, Microsoft has published the results of its study concerning users' ability to focus on what is displayed. In 2000, it was valued at more than 12 seconds, while it was equal to 8 seconds in 2016. A decrease of 25% that keeps going through time.

Here is a graph that illustrates this data:

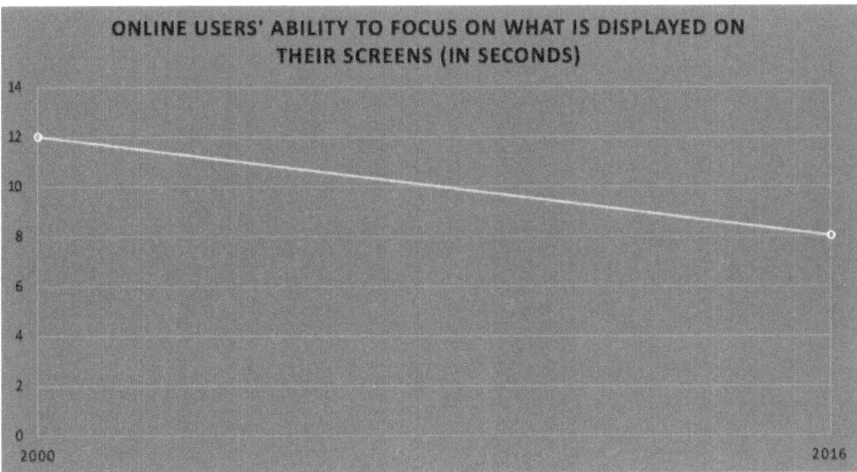

This shows the importance of social medias in pushing prospects to buy a product / service. It is due to our senses, and therefore our imagination.

With the evolution of digital commerce, it becomes much easier and faster to find whatever someone is looking for.

Considering social medias, Facebook offers the possibility to marketers of creating advertisings depending on several particular criteria: age, gender, geographical location, interests or even their behavior on the social network. Companies are able to target a specific part of the population that is very likely to proceed to a purchase of goods / services.

In the United States, digital advertising spending has increased by 110% between 2016 and 2020, jumping to 151,29 billion dollars (eMarketers.com).

Here is a graph that illustrates this data:

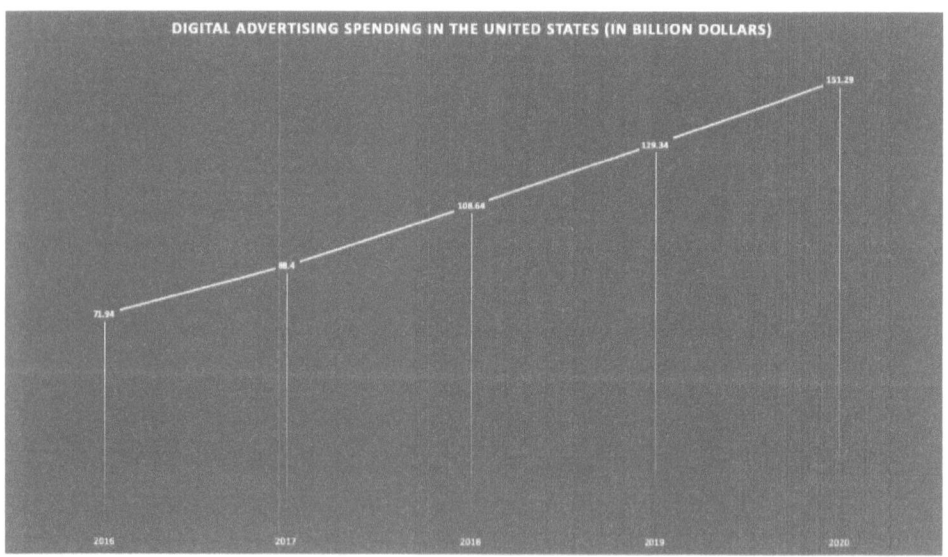

DIGITAL ADVERTISING SPENDING IN THE UNITED STATES (IN BILLION DOLLARS)

The reason? Companies are aware of the fact that the first times a customer sees an advertising of their goods or services are the most important. As a consequence, a huge budget is spent on this aspect of their expansionary strategy. This is what marketers call the "Rule of 7".

This marketing principle states that a company's prospects need to come across its promotional campaign at least seven times before noticing it and starting taking action. Therefore, those seven first times are the most crucial moments for a company when promoting its services or goods. And in order to notice advertisings, our senses are stimulated: radio (hearing), TV (hearing and sight), advertising board (sight)…

The next step for those companies it to push the customer, who has money to spend, to think that the advertised product is useful enough to execute what marketers call the "target action".

When we see an advertisement on the Internet, we often come across a "Buy" button.

It can also be displayed as:

* ❖ "Register".

* ❖ Or "Add to Cart" for instance.

The former would allow the company to send regular emails to its prospects concerning its new discounts, and new products. On the other side, collecting data on who added products to their cart would allow them re-target online users who are the most likely to buy from that store, since adding to the cart is the first step in the purchase process.

Every single company can create a marketing campaign for a specific aim, which is the "target action". All of them are related to generating money by attracting people to their product / service.

When doing an advertisement, brands are aware that it may be something completely new for people who will watch it. Therefore, they use the reproductive power of imagination.

Since imagination is the pivot of the thought process (according to Aristotle), it's the most important human faculty to target.

Once imagination has been directed to perceive the benefits a product can provide the customer, the latter's thought will push him / her to purchase it. This is the process that leads to compulsive purchases.

People may not need that specific service / object, but by "manipulating" their senses, marketing experts push them to actually think that they should buy it. They end up doing so, thanks to imagination.

As declared by the empiricist philosopher David Hume in *"An Enquiry Concerning Human Understanding"*, "all belief of a matter of fact, or real existence, is derived merely from some object, present to the memory or senses, and a customary conjunction between that and some other object".

What does this set out? Simply that, when a person tries the advertised product once and sees that it works, she gets "accustomed" to the habit of purchasing that particular object. Namely, she becomes a "customer".

If we sum up all the aspects related to the notion of "imagination" that we have seen until now, we can say that imagination pushes prospects purchase a particular product through senses.

Also, we can add Stoics' statement according to which imagination can be influenced by our emotions, and therefore it can have an impact on our thoughts, as well as on our perception of an advertised service / object (associating it with positive emotions).

Scenario to understand compulsive shopping

Let's take the following example. A random worker named Georges is accustomed to a gym (let's name it Top Fit) near his home, and a fast-food has just established near this sport center. Georges follows Top Fit's Facebook page, which allows the newly established brand target him through digital advertisings.

As a consequence, that person may feel keen to try it once because of the process we have described until now (senses, imagination, thoughts). Once that purchase becomes a habit, Georges will associate going to the gym to having a meal at that particular fast-food. A kind of causal relationship will be established in Georges' mind.

In Georges' mind, training at Top Fit induces eating at the newly-established fast-food

This is the time when the prospect quickly jumps from "one-time-shopper" to the "customer" box. This is what we call compulsive shopping.

It's an essential notion in Marketing that is defined by investopedia.com as an "unhealthy obsession with shopping that interferes with the daily life of the afflicted". Also, it explains that it has a psychological aspect that creates the "need to shop, even unwanted items". It's related to the fact that the consumer identifies himself, or herself, to that specific object or service thanks to the branding policy that the company's marketing experts have led. We'll talk more in depth about this aspect in the second part of this eBook.

Marketing experts are aware of the fact that the humankind will never be as satisfied as the first time trying a product, which will push him/her to buy it as many times as possible at a huge frequency. Companies will always earn money by giving its customers the hope that they will experience that feeling again, which is mostly false. To achieve this, they stimulate their prospects' senses to make them think that purchasing the service / object will provide them with that pleasant feeling.

Fabian Dorsch, in the "*Routledge Handbook of Philosophy of Imagination*", performs a 10 pages long philosophy analysis of David Hume's perception about the notion of imagination. The empiricist philosopher distinguishes three types of ideas: ideas of judgment / of fancy / of memory. All three types of idea differ in vivacity, identified as "assent", which is divided in five different features.

The third feature that is evoked is the "impact on causal / functional role of the episodes concerned". The example given by Fabian Dorsch to illustrate Hume's statement is the situation when we see a child in danger. In that situation, we will tend to save him.

It's the same scheme when the imaginary person we mentioned previously, Georges, will see price cuts at the fast-food where he used to have dinner after gym.

His consumer inner spirit will be swiftly keyed up by the display of promotions.

As a consequence, that person will be keen to buy it, even if no pleasure is generated. These are impulsive purchases.

The importance of price-cuts in compulsive purchasing behavior

According to Kahneman and Tversky's research shared in 1979 concerning human behavior and price marketing campaigns (*"Théorie des prospects généralisée aux comparaisons multi-attributs"*), the humankind's perceptual apparel is more adapted to evaluating changes rather than the object's real value.

Furthermore, these price-cuts have even more impact when they are done at a precise frequency. Indeed, Aradhna Krishna, an American academic known for its writings focused on marketing, affirmed that firms have to keep a close-eye to the competitors' promotions in order to conduct a correct promotional policy (*"Effect of Dealing Patterns on Consumer Perceptions of Deal Frequency and Willingness to Pay"*, 1991). A time-limited discount in the gym's membership price may be accompanied by a promotion at the fast-food, and vice-versa.

What is important in imagination and thought interdependence is that the former creates detachment with reality (thanks to emotions) while thoughts aren't threatened by emotions. Stoics agree with this philosophy, saying that phantasia, referred to as "creative imagination" nowadays, is the center of our thoughts / language. Language can take two shapes: written or spoken.

This is the reason why the key to successful marketing campaigns is the manipulation of imagination. The idea is to associate positive emotions to that product / service. Namely, seeing a fast-food advertisement after coming out from gym will create positive emotions and feelings. This is the result of two characteristics of the prospect.

The first one is that the latter is hungry, and is seeking something to eat. Humankind can have great resolutions, yet do two things with totally opposite effects. This fact can be illustrated with the habit of smoking, which is bad for health. Yet, over 5.7 trillion cigarettes were smoked worldwide in 2016 (according to tobaccoatlas.org). Our emotions and feelings have serious consequences on our purchasing behavior, and therefore also on our decision-making.

This brings about what we refer to as the "impulsive buying behavior". We'll begin with branding, and perception in general.

Impulsive Purchasing Behavior

Branding

"Branding", as a general marketing concept, is defined as the "marketing practice of creating a name, symbol or design that identifies and differentiates a product from other products" (entrepreneur.com).

Impulsive purchasing behavior is triggered by emotions and feelings. Here comes the role of "emotional branding". It is defined as "the consumer's attachment of a strong, specific, usage-relevant emotion such as Bonding, Companionship, or love to the brand" (John Rossiter, Steve Bellamn, *Emotional Branding Pays Off*, 2012).

It's the identity of a particular brand that will differentiate it from others. Does it provide us with low-quality or high-quality products? What about the costs? Is it a low-cost or high-cost company? The aim is to create an image of the company in the consumer's brain to make him, or her, remember and recognize the brand when seeing it or hearing about its product category ("Rule of 7").

To illustrate the importance of branding, we'll take the example of Apple.

Case Study 1: Apple's branding philosophy

Created in 1976 by Ronald Wayne, Steve Wozniak and Steve Jobs in the latter's garage, Apple is a true icon of American capitalism. It is the first private company in history to reach a value of $ 1 trillion on the stock market. The world-famous American magazine "*Fortune*" has ranked the company as the most admired one in the world during 7 consecutive years, from 2006 to 2013.

She owes this great success to her branding. As a nod to the famous René Descartes cogito "I think, therefore I am", Apple used "iThink, therefore iMac" in 1998 to promote the iMac. Including the concept of the person within each of its products, Apple seeks the feeling of identity and assimilation of the customer to its products: iMac, iPod, iPad, iPhone, iWatch…

Its branding philosophy is so powerful at the point that an iPhone owner won't tell you that he can't find his smartphone, but he would rather ask if you have seen his "iPhone".

Many strategies are put into practice, including the association of white headphones with its devices or the rectangular shape of its products' boxes that are proudly brandished by their followers right out of the new range.

In addition to pushing people invest in that company's stocks, which brings revenues, it instills a sense of belonging created by notoriety and corporate culture. This is what lets some companies charge more than other similar unbranded companies that are on the same market.

At a worldwide socioeconomic change period, YBWA/Chiat/Day opted for "Think different" as Apple's slogan in 1997. In addition to the grey logo that symbolizes modernism and technology, the branding of Apple is accentuated with its slogan: thinking outside the box and being a creative person who brings modern ideas by using Apple's technology. It was the rise of multiculturalism and alternative media, and the context was perfect for Steve Job's company to conquer this growing juicy market.

The importance is branding is such that Apple has designed six different logos to get to the current one. Innovation is a key concept in branding as a general notion.

According to a neuroscientist at the University of Oxford, Sundeep Teki, our brains are "genetically wired to seek needs such as security and social status". The feeling of being seen as "inferior" to others because of the fact that a person doesn't own the newest iPhone is real.

Also, the role of YouTube stars as influencers became even more preponderant with the release of iPhone X in 2019. Apple chose to conquer this expansionary market, also known as "brand marketing".

An experiment driven by Stefan Zak and Maria Hasprova, both searches at the University of Economics in Bratislava, showed that 32.8% of the respondents consider the products promoted by influencers to be high of quality and that 21.9% of the plotted population stated that they were encouraged to execute the target action. Apple, and brands in general, is aware that influencers' role isn't to neglect.

An influencer has notoriety over his, or her, community. Several types of feelings can be allocated to these public figures, in particular confidence, excitement, admiration and many others... Human beings are subject to their emotions and feelings, which lead to impulsive purchases.

Another example of brand marketing is Coke.

Case Study 2: Coke's branding philosophy

Coke has notoriety because of its identity that was cultivated over time. With a so-called "magic formula", Coca-Cola has managed to create a myth around its product. PepsiCo has developed a product that tastes very similar to Coke's. Yet, it wasn't enough to convince the "American Way of Life" icon company's customers to purchase its soda rather the latter's.

With a more focused business model than Pepsi on beverage, Coca-Cola had a higher market share than Pepsi between 2008 and 2018 (Beverage Digest). We will put this success into perspective by focusing on the branding aspect of Coke.

As explained by Forbes, a "lasting imprint" has to be created on the consumer's consciousness through consistency and a homogeneous advertising policy, meaning promoting campaigns that look similar through time. Coca-Cola has kept similar marketing features: happy and smiling people and some simple taglines. The slogan "Taste the feeling" attracted the brand's confidence, and is used since 2009.

Through customers' senses, Coke aims to assimilate its brand to a fresh soda which can be drank on different occasions, especially during Christmas meals.

During the 1930s, soft drinks were very seasonal, with winter being the least favorable season for the consumption of Coca-Cola. The American soda company will therefore not hesitate to assimilate their name to that of the world-famous character "Santa Claus". During his long nights in the course of delivering his gifts, nothing was better than a cold drink with a very joyful look.

This is how Coca-Cola cultivated a "lasting imprint", as *Forbes* would qualify it, to remain in its customers' mind. By making of Santa Claus its best ambassador, Coke made us feel a need for this drink for successful parties. This way, families won't celebrate Christmas without this drink, and this will generate consequent revenues.

Satyendra Singh, in *"Impact of Color on Marketing"*, stated that "colors evoke brands", adding that "the high importance placed on color is an acknowledgment of manufacturers' understanding that color has strong emotional loading".

In the case of Coca-Cola, red is "associated with increasing metabolic state" (Satyendra Singh). Meaning that, in the case of food, it's a source of energy. Therefore, customers would perceive as a highly energetic beverage. This is the factor that triggers impulsive purchases.

After taking more than a decade of loss, Coca Cola launched a worldwide marketing campaign named "Share a Coca Cola". In opposite to its two main competitors, Pepsi and Dr. Pepper (both remaining in loss), Coke recorded an increase of 0,4% in its total sales between June and August 2014 compared to the ones at the same period a year before in the United States.

This idea was first tested in Australia in 2011, with 50 000 forenames printed on its cans. Youth didn't hesitate to share pictures of their soda on the social medias with their name printed on it, doing a free advertising for the red soda company. The company even selected three names that would be considered as "rare", which were even sold on platforms such as eBay or Amazon for dozens of dollars. A huge success! This way, Coke would remain in its customers' mind when looking for a soda in supermarkets.

Perception

According to Immanuel Kant, the human mind in general is based on its perception of the facts, not on the actual facts. This is the meaning of "representation". Impulsive buyers will follow this trend. Aristotle's *"De Anima, book 3, Part3"* states that imagination is part of thinking (based on senses, as we said at the beginning), but also of perception. This is an extremely important characteristic of imagination.

Kant's belief can be supported by David Hume's in *"Routledge of Philosophy of Imagination"* (Chapter 3, Section 2), where he declares that the humankind doesn't have control on its sight, but that it has control over its perception. Just like the example given saying that we can "paint someone without needing him to exist", we can see an object that we don't need and perceive it as something to purchase just because of our ability of controlling this faculty. The aim of advertisements is to push us perceive the object we see as a "need".

The notion "principle of marketing" is defined as a process "by which a consumer identifies, organizes, and interprets information to create meaning" (oer2go.org). Isn't it extremely important in the machinery that will push the customer to execute the "target action", through an impulsive purchasing behavior?

Perception is a human faculty that occupies a central role for marketing experts. In addition to the promotion of the product / service itself, it's also the promotion of a particular picture of the service / product that is made by the companies. When leading a promotional campaign, marketing experts aim to project a particular perception of the product / service to the customer. Perception's role is absolutely not negligible.

If our imagination provides us with positive ideas / judgments concerning that specific service / product, then we'll think about it positively. It will create positive emotions. As a consequence, we'll be keen to purchase it.

To sum up…

Imagination plays an extremely important in both compulsive and impulsive purchasing behaviors. Imagination is the product of senses, and it allows us to think (Aristotle). Obsessions are thoughts, images or ideas that a person isn't able to stop thinking about, causing him, or her, to feel anxious. Compulsions are the behaviors that humans engage to put an end to these obsessions. Therefore, the latter depend on imagination. On the other hand, impulsive buying behavior is the consequence of our emotions, which in turn, are subject to our perception. Aristotle declares, in *De Anima, book 3, Part3*, that imagination is part of perception. According to the Immanuel Kant, human mind is usually based on "the perception of the facts", not on the actual facts (*Kant's Theory of the Imagination*). Since the humankind has control over its perception, it has to remain the main focus of marketers. This is the reason why imagination is a preponderant factor in successful marketing campaigns.

Copyright © 2020 by Balbacha El Mehdi.

All rights reserved. No part of this book may be reproduced or used in any manner without written permission of the copyright owner except for the use of quotations in a book review. For more information, address: mehdi.balbacha1@gmail.com

FIRST EDITION

www.ingramcontent.com/pod-product-compliance
Lightning Source LLC
Chambersburg PA
CBHW031510210526
45463CB00008B/3174

979865119712 5